To my son, Tuhui, who is the raindrop that renewed my world and grew it in so many new and beautiful ways.
May everything we do together continue to honor our ancestors while healing the world for our future generations. —N.H.

For Emily and Bill, Stephanie, Donald, and Ethel; to my friend Nick and his beautiful work;
and to all those who protect and grow native plants and care for our earth —J.W.

To my grandad Chris, whose abundant love and wisdom have helped me grow into the person I am today —M.G.

Library of Congress Control Number: 2023940670
ISBN 978-0-06-322128-4

Typography by Chelsea C. Donaldson
24 25 26 27 28 RTLO 10 9 8 7 6 5 4 3 2 1

First Edition

Nicholas Hummingbird

Can You Hear the Plants Speak?

with Julia Wasson

illustrations by
Madelyn Goodnight

HARPER
An Imprint of HarperCollins Publishers

Our people believe spirit lives in everything.
Mountain, river, wind, tree.

Come take a walk with me.

I spent long summer days with my great-grandparents, exploring every rock and plant, learning when the creeks ran and the plants flowered.

I chased squirrels,
    played with lizards,

stared down rattlesnakes.

Wind sang through bunchgrasses,
woodpecker tapped his heartbeat,
leaves danced across the ground.

We listened as our plant relatives spoke.

Wild strawberries: *We'll quench your thirst when the streams run dry.*

Buckwheat: *Birds eat my seeds, and so can you.*

White sage: *My smoke will lift your prayers to heaven.*

We rested in Grandfather Oak's shade. "These trees are our ancestors. They give us our food, our medicine, our connection to spirit," my great-grandparents explained. "And we thank them with a song, a blessing, a few drops of water."

I sprinkled cool water as my great-grandparents quietly hummed an ancient song.

I felt their song inside me.

But not everyone could hear plants speak.
Some people thought our lands would be
more useful flattened in concrete.

The land was silenced.

I grew up, and the city grew, too.
When my great-grandparents passed, I lost their voices.

Adrift, I was lost, too.

But wait, who's this?

Monarch at rest on milkweed, emerging through a crack. Milkweed's scent whispered:

Don't give up.

I remembered my great-grandparents' voices, singing in the shade of Grandfather Oak.

Thank you, brother, I whispered.

I had to find a way to keep their voices alive.

But the cities were so big, the natural places so few.

What could one person do?

I listened.

A drop of rain splashed in the dry dust, where thirsty seeds waited.

That one drop might germinate one seed.

One drop, then many.

The sharp scent of creosote rose. I felt the seeds drink.

I knew what to do.

Thank you, I whispered to the sky and the plants.

From one, I would grow many.

I had so much to learn.

Plants became my best teachers:

Black walnut: *Gather our hard, round shells and chill us for the winter.*

Poppy: *Shake our seeds into baskets as winds scatter them.*

Juncus: *Divide our stems after fledglings leave their nests.*

Lupine: *We carpet the hillsides. Our seed coats are broken by a tumble of rock.*

Palo verde: *My seeds pass through ravens' stomachs; soften me with acid.*

Manzanita: *We bloom after wildfire. Wake our seeds with a wisp of smoke.*

And then my son is born. I name him Tuhui,
our word for the drop of rain that starts the seed.

We draw strength from wind and mountain, bobcat and hummingbird, bringing life to our home in the city.

We grow plants for all our relatives.

Each new seedling is a healing. Tiny neighbors check them out.

"Grow strong, little guys; you're the hope of so many!"

We plant empty places.

"This is how we give back. These oaks will shade our grandchildren,"
I explain, just as my great-grandparents had explained to me.

"Can you hear the plants speak?" I ask Tuhui.

"Yes."

"What do they tell you?"

"They say thank you."

And the song grows.
In him, in me, and maybe in you.

Listen.

Can you hear it?

What We Can Do

Did you know plants can go extinct—just like dinosaurs?

When plants lose their habitat, they can go extinct. The bees, birds, and animals that depend on those plants can go extinct also.

But we *can* help.

Learn to Look

Start by paying attention. I've always been curious. "Look," my great-grandparents would say, "Nick gets into everything! Just like a hummingbird!" I remember how they taught me to be gentle, to smell a plant by softly touching a leaf and letting the fragrant oils rub off on my finger.

Now I learn from spending time in natural parks, preserves, even empty lots with plants growing.

You can find these places, too. Stop, sit down, relax, and open your senses. Let the plants, pollinators, and animals who live there show you their world. Notice scents, textures, and colors. Search for pollinators and observe them at work. You might enjoy recording your findings in a sketchbook or journal. Use plant ID books, native plant websites, and apps to learn about what you see. Maybe you can contribute to insect or bird counts through your natural history museum.

Take Action

Grow a native plant at home.

On our small apartment balcony, Tuhui and I provide relief for the monarch butterflies facing extinction. Their caterpillars only eat milkweed leaves, so we grow it for them. We also grow yarrow and coastal sunflowers that make nectar that the adult monarchs drink. Now butterflies visit our third story. Even songbirds find us! One day, Tuhui said, "I hear a bird!" It was a bushtit, swirling and swinging upside down from the branches of our manzanita.

Try these tips with a grown-up helper:

- If you don't have a yard, try growing on a balcony or windowsill.

- Try to find local nurseries selling native seeds and plants. Local nurseries can help you learn which plants will flourish at your home or schoolyard and what they need to stay healthy.

- Observe your space throughout the day. Notice sun and shade, then match the plants to your space. For instance, if your space is sunny, don't try to grow plants that like to be under trees.

- For balconies or windowsills, get the largest containers you can, then choose plants whose roots will have room to grow.

- Cactus mix combined with perlite has fewer chemicals than potting soil. Add fertilizer during your plants' growing season.

- In containers, your plants' roots won't be able to grow down to find water deep in the earth—you'll have to provide it. You may need to water every day during hot weather to keep the soil from drying out. But don't water if the soil feels soggy: If the soil is too wet, the roots won't be able to breathe.

- Take time to enjoy your plants, listen to them, and see who comes to visit!

Books for adults:

Kimmerer, Robin Wall. *Braiding Sweetgrass: Indigenous Wisdom, Scientific Knowledge, and the Teachings of Plants.* Milkweed Editions, 2015.

Tallamy, Douglas W. *Bringing Nature Home: How You Can Sustain Wildlife with Native Plants* (Updated and Expanded). Timber Press, 2009.

Books for students:

Schaefer, Lola M., and Adam Schaefer. *Because of an Acorn.* Chronicle Books, 2016.

Tripp. Analisa. *A Is for Acorn: A California Indian ABC.* Heyday Books, 2015.